Essence

AF624470

H.M Hussain

BookLeaf Publishing

Presentation by *BookLeaf Publishing*

Web: www.bookleafpub.com

E-mail: info@bookleafpub.com

ISBN: 9789357445450

First edition 2022

DEDICATION

For Maryem

ACKNOWLEDGEMENT

I want to thank everyone who has been part of this journey long before I embarked on this challenge. I owe a huge debt of gratitude to Gail Low, Kirsty Gunn, Beth McDonough, and the late Eddie Small who all helped me become the writer I am today.

I want to thank Rebecca Baird for bringing this opportunity to my attention. Thank you for your honesty, your friendship, and unwavering support.

Thank you to my parents, partner, friends, and family who cheer me on in everything I do.

Thank you to the team at Book Leaf Publishing for making my debut collection possible.

PREFACE

The Erasure poems in Rudy Francisco's book *I'll Fly Away* inspired this collection, and the technique used within.

Candy by Paolo Nutini

i)

I perched
myself
with the
most
heartless
and helpless one.

Your skin
just
lay
false, defeated.

My name,
quite
rough,
bathed and washed,
lay
on some
writings

for you.

It was waiting -
waiting for you,

showing jagged ends,
feeling cheap,
wearing a mimicry of halos.

That's all they do;
is
cut throats.

All of them
limp atop the
angels,
restless,
they keep me waiting and wanting.

ii)

I perched

heartless
and helpless.

Your skin
lay
Defeated.

My name
washed
you.

Jagged ends
feeling cheap,
a mimicry.
Restless
me, waiting and wanting.

iii)

Perched,
heartless,
helpless.
Your skin
defeated
my name.

Feeling cheap,
restless,
waiting and wanting.

iv)

Perched,
heartless,
helpless.

Skin-defeated,
feeling cheap,
restless
and wanting.

Covid-19 Test Receipt Card

i)

Your name
mixed up,
to control the positive touch recent contacts have.
Take anyone you have met and place the details back.

You need the free call at your rate.

ii)

Free at your rate.

Take anyone you have met.
Control the touch - mixed up
when speaking your name.

iii)

Free rate.

You
control the mixed up
speaking of your name

iv)

Control the speaking of
your name.

Offer Letter

i)

On you an offer,
an outline.

We own a bit of worth.

These vest
a year all
and all.

After you, additional
projects simply reboot.

Adoption; leave
12,
balance
new.

Offering
enhanced
insurance is
responsible.

Life:
provide assurance once they pass.
Does a member of our
loved ones pay times
to a named kin?

Wellbeing,
wellbeing
your whole self.

Quarterly.

Review every quarter we
recognise –
grow.
Under the scheme you can - free-free
a moment here.

With you
our date is
further to me!

ii)

An offer,
an outline,
a bit of worth,
- a year all
and all.

After, you simply reboot.

Enhanced
insurance.

Life:
assurance
they pass.
A member of times
to a named kin.

Wellbeingwellbeing
your whole self
every quarter.

Under the scheme
a moment
with you
is
further to me.

iii)

An offer
worth
a
simply
enhanced
life.

Pass-times
to a kin.

Wellbeing -
every
moment
with you
is
me.

iv)

Worth
simply
enhanced
Life.

To a kin
every
moment
with you
is.

v)

Simply-
every
moment:

you.

Random Wikipedia Article

i)

Created by
many between
various affairs,
War remained. So there are
conversations in dialect, in a tavern.
in later years most monologue pieces
widely remembered, originated lasting sayings:
Supreme returns.

To replace similar analogue, objected
the garrulous: speak in
an unfashionable freedom of expression -
standard.

The first years made elsewhere.

a rapidly rising
detailed
lips, a portrait ethnic,
unparalleled.

wider wartime
soon
gained acclaim.
Trouble finding time,
resurrection in the
obscure part due to barrier for potential.

ii)

Created
between
various affairs,
War remained in a tavern.

In years most monologue pieces
originated
Supreme.

To
the garrulous,
an unfashionable freedom of expression
made elsewhere
a
detailed
portrait -
unparalleled

Soon,
time,
the
obscure barrier, fought for potential.

iii)

Various affairs remained.
A tavern,
in pieces,
originated
Supreme.

The
unfashionable expression
made a
detailed
portrait
unparalleled.

Soon,
time
fought for potential.

iv)

Various affairs in pieces
originated.

The
expression
made
time
for potential.

v)

In
time
for potential.

@hmhussain21

i)

Yes, another life. the

excited
in

#boxing #writing #readingcommunity

Inshallah!

Spiderman!!!

Thank you
for the invite! Make sure to join us on Sunday.

ii)

Yes, another life.

excited.

#writing

Inshallah!

the invite! join us on Sunday.

iii)

Another life,
excited -
writing
'Inshallah!'

Invite us on Sunday.

iv)

Life?

Inshallah.

That View (an original poem)

i)

I love this part the most, the last leg of the
journey, a final five minutes.
I've been sitting in the same seat for four hours,
legs stiffening and cramping.
But the view that unfolds before me makes it
worth it.

There is nothing quite like the feeling of being in
a train that is rolling across the
Tay Rail Bridge, over the river as the small city
comes into view. In the distance the monument
at the Law, a beacon of welcome – home is in
sight now. At the foot of the Law sits the rest of
the city, low and humble.

ii)

This part, the last leg - final
four hours.
The view that unfolds.
before it - nothing.
like rolling river,
the distance:
welcome
sight
of rest, low and humble.

iii)

This last leg.
Four hours
the view unfolds,
like rolling river,
the distance
welcome.

iv)

Four hours
the view unfolds -
welcome

Parents' Eyes (an original poem)

i)

If I look into my mother's
eyes, will I see her beloved
Lahore?
I think it nestles in the creases
around her lids, just like her father's –
the same black marks, the same unconditional
love,
the same never letting go.

And if I look into my father's, both open and
closed,
will I see empty space, cool whites, like the
liminal
in-between of airports that fill the gap
between here and there?

ii)

Look, my mother's
eyes see her beloved.
The creases
around her lids
marks unconditional love.
never letting go.

And my father's, both open and closed,
see empty space, the liminal
that fill the gap
between here and there.

iii)

My
eyes see
the creases
around her
unconditional love.
'Never go.'

And my
empty space (liminal)
fill the
here and there.

iv)
Creases
around
love
never go.

Empty space
here and there.

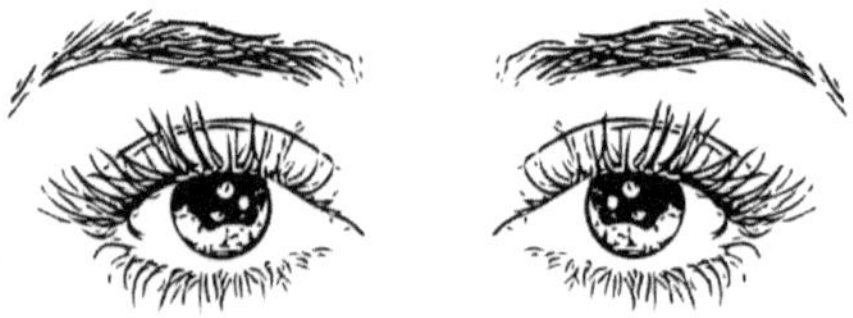

The Rat, The Beggar & The Smoker (an original poem)

i)

Park Lane winds to the left.
Next to the kerb lies dead
a rat; grey, brown, with red.

Its tail curls limply behind,
entrails making tarmac their bed.

Mouth and eyes open. I stop
in a mixture of disgust,
intrigue
and sadness.

Flies have started
their rounds, two, three
four;

Too many to count.
I move along.

Chicken restaurant,
takeaways, barbers, grocers
and Tesco.

A dread-headed man sits
disheveled next to the
oversized Costa cup,
his own empty in hand.

A King book
always half open,
bin bags piling,
an old shoe; not his.

Redbrick eye-sores, doors crammed like
too many teeth, discoloured and
different.

On the step of number 18,
every morning
she sits pyjama'd, long black coat,
and scraped back hair.
an ever-burning cigarette in hand,
quivering. Face sunken,
dragged down by the bags beneath her eyes,
she smiles, bearing all front teeth.

Somewhere, between entrails and front teeth,
I lose my thoughts.
but I find them daily:
the rat,
the beggar
&
the smoker.

As sure as my next step hitting the ground.

Days pass - the rat,
flattened to dust
and bones

The beggar,
more pleasant, cup still empty.

The smoker, closer to death,
with no sign of showing.

ii)

Winds left
the dead
limply behind.
Entrails.
Mouth and eyes open. I stop
in disgust,
intrigue
and sadness.

Two, three
four;
too many to count.
move along.

A dread-headed man
dishevelled,empty in hand.

A king half open,
an old shoe; not his.

Crammed like
too many teeth, discoloured
scraped back.
ever-burning
sunken,
dragged down by eyes

bearing all.

Somewhere,
I lose my thoughts
daily:
the
ground
flattened to dust
and
empty.

death
with no sign of showing.

iii)

Left
the dead
behind.

Entrails - too many to
move along.

Dread-headed,
dishevelled,
empty in hand.

Half-open

scraped back,
Ever-burning -
sunken eyes
bearing all.

Somewhere,
the flattened dust,
empty
death
showing.

iv)

The dead
entrails
move along,
disheveled,
bearing all.

Somewhere,
empty death,
showing.

v)

The
disheveled
bearing
empty death.

Home Lines (an original poem)

take a line,
- - - - - - - - - soft
---------- or hard,
a wall even;
and set it between two.

me & you

watch it give shelter to words:

us
them
home
invasion
belonging
and stealing.

The Art of Writing (an original poem)

i)

The art of writing is quite hard to master.
When that white stares back – where to begin?
God, this piece is already a disaster.
Write what you know of life and the hereafter,
Of the good in this world, and decaying sin.
Holy shit, writing is hard to master.
A lightning idea strikes; to type, type faster.
For like thirty seconds until you blank again.
Right, I'll tidy my desk, it's a pure disaster.
Coffee break! – black drink make write smarter.
Title and first image down, every word is a win.
Who said the art of writing was hard to master?
Get it all down, all the crap – edit after.
Hmm what shall call him? I think Flynn.
What happens next? Nuclear bomb or natural
disaster?
Okay that'll do – tomorrow will be better.
By noon I'll be two thousand words in.
Pfft! this writing thing isn't hard to master.
I think I'll call this one 'The Art of Disaster'.

ii)

The art master
stares back – already a disaster.
'Life
Of the good in decaying sin,
holy Master.'
Lightning strikes
for thirty seconds, again
pure disaster.

Every word
hard to master.
all I think:
What next? Disaster?
Tomorrow,
by noon, I'll master
this disaster.

iii)

The master
already a disaster.

Pure disaster - every word
hard to master.

What next? Disaster?

Tomorrow
I'll master
this disaster.

iv)

Master
every word.
To master
Tomorrow
I'll master
this disaster.

v)

To master
tomorrow
master
this.

Heroes (an original poem)

i)

When I was six years old, I wanted to be
Superman.
I wanted to fly,
to be super strong and fast.

I wanted that thick lock of hair to curl
down my forehead.
I also wanted to be Hercules.
Super strong with armour and a sword.

When I was eight, I wanted to be Spiderman.
I loved the thought of swinging
between buildings and climbing walls.
My mum even made a homemade mask that I
drew webbing on with a black felt-tip pen.
I made spiders crawl onto my hand hoping that
they would bite me and I would transform.
I wanted to be a spy, a Jedi, and a world
champion boxer like Muhammad Ali.

Now I'm 28 years-old and I don't know who my heroes are.
But I know they're not
from Krypton.
They don't swing swords, or
leap from tall buildings.

I no longer wait
to be super by accident.
I run through scenarios faster than a speeding bullet.
I web up insecurities.
I jab, weave and brawl
through twelve rounds of uncertainty
a day.

And raise my hand in victory when failure hasn't knocked
me out for the count.

ii)

Six years-old, I wanted to be Superman.
wanted to fly,
be super strong and fast.
To be Hercules.
Super strong with armour and sword.
Eight:

swinging
between buildings, climbing walls.

A homemade mask I drew webbing on.
made spiders crawl onto my hand -
bite me and I transform.
I wanted to be a spy, a Jedi, and a world
champion boxer like Muhammad Ali.

Now, 28 years-old and I don't know my heroes.
they're not
from Krypton.
Don't swing swords, or
leap tall buildings.

I no longer wait
to be super.
I run scenarios faster than a bullet.
web up insecurities.
I jab, weave and brawl
twelve rounds of uncertainty
a day.

And raise my hand in victory when failure hasn't
knocked
me out.

iii)

Six years-old, Superman
wanted to fly,
be super strong and fast.

Super!

A mask I drew on
made me transform.

28 years-old and… I don’t know.

I wait
to be super.

Web up insecurities.
jab, weave and brawl
rounds of uncertainty.

Raise my hand in victory when failure hasn’t
knocked
me out.

iv)

Wanted to
be super strong.

A mask
made me.

I don't
wait
to be super.

Insecurities.
weave
rounds of uncertainty.

Raise my hand in victory when failure hasn't
knocked
me out.

v)

Don’t
wait
to be super.

Raise hand in victory.

Failure hasn’t knocked
me out.

Homemaking (an original poem)

i)

I thought I knew what 'home' was.
Home is origin, The place I'm from.
Dundee; where family and friends are
the place I always return to,
the place I know best.

Walking through the streets knowing where
everything is; my flat
university campus,
learning how to take up space
in this city.

The city centre; cafes, takeaways and
restaurants,
where memories of home have formed.
But I will leave
and create another elsewhere.
To appreciate home I must experience
its absence, what it is to leave.
This will always be here to welcome me back.

to this leave-taking happened earlier
As I sat in Leeds where I worked for six weeks.

'Home' was my place of rest, where I ate, where
I prayed, where I retired at the end of the day;
the things we do when at home.
The large, tower block, I took the bare room and
began populating it.
Pockets; wallet, spare change, keys, receipts,
scraps of paper –
performing the same acts in Dundee.
I unpacked clothes, easily stored in the small
wardrobe.
migrant objects, like me, were living somewhere
new.

Ready to house my displaced objects; books,
reusable coffee cup, a 'good luck' card
equipment for the gym and some toiletries.
This ritual; cheap, false.
This place, a place barely 'home', a 'step-home'.
It was a make-believe house, a game
much like 'playing housies' as a child.
Doing just that, but alone.
objects in space helped make sense of my new
home,
helped visualise how I would use the space.
With my belongings, I made anonymous space
my own,

planted signifiers of my identity within
cupboards, drawers and the bathroom.
My experience of home a template
a home not only for myself but things
which were an extension of me.
filled the space, made it familiar,
making the unknown identifiable.
traces of ‘home things’ in this new dwelling
weren’t enough. the white walls, the
not-enough-stuff, or
no one to share the space with.
Try as I might,
the space still felt as owner-less as a hotel room.

ii)

I thought I knew ‘home’.
Origin, the place I’m from.
Where family and friends are,
the place I always return to,
the place I know.

The streets; knowing where
to take up space
in this city.
where memories have formed.
But I leave
and create elsewhere home -

I must experience
absence, leave
to welcome me back.
Leave-taking happened.
As I sat in Leeds where
'home' was my place of rest, where I ate,
prayed, retired at the end of the day;

things we do at home.
I took the bare room, began populating it.
pockets; wallet, spare change, keys, receipts,
scraps of paper –
the same acts in Dundee.
Unpacked clothes, easily stored
migrant objects, like me, living somewhere new.

I filled this house with my displaced objects;
books,
re-useable coffee cup, a 'good luck' card
equipment for the gym, toiletries.
This ritual place, a barely 'home' / 'step-home'.
A make-believe house, a game
much like a child,
but alone.
Objects in space make sense of home
visualise the space,
my belongings,
I made anonymous space my own,
planted signifiers of identity within

template.
Home:
an extension of me.
Filled the space, made it familiar;
the unknown identifiable.
Traces of 'home things' in new dwelling
weren't enough.
white walls, the not-enough-stuff, or
no one to share with.
Space as owner-less as a hotel room.

iii)

I thought I knew 'home'.
origin, the place I'm from.
Where family and friends are
the place I always return to
the place I know.

The streets; knowing where
to take up space
in this city.
Where memories have formed.
But I leave
and create elsewhere home -
I must experience
absence, leave
to welcome me back.
Leave-taking happened

as I sat in Leeds where
'home' was my place of rest, where I ate,
prayed, retired at the end of the day;

Things we do at home.
I took the bare room, began populating it.
pockets; wallet, spare change, keys, receipts,
scraps of paper –
the same acts in Dundee.
Unpacked clothes, easily stored
migrant objects, like me, living somewhere new.

House my displaced objects; books,
re-useable coffee cup, a 'good luck' card
equipment for the gym, toiletries.
This ritual place, a barely 'home' / 'step-home'.
a make-believe house, a game
much like a child,
but alone.
Objects in space make sense of home
visualise the space,
my belongings.
I made anonymous space my own,
planted signifiers of identity within
template.
Home:
an extension of me.
Filled the space, made it familiar;
the unknown identifiable.

traces of ‘home things’ in new dwelling
weren’t enough.
white walls, the not-enough-stuff, or
no one share with.
space as owner-less as a hotel room.

iv)

‘Home’.
origin,
where family and friends are,
the place I always return to.

Knowing where
to take up space,
where memories have formed.
I leave
and create elsewhere home -
experience
absence.

Leave-taking…

‘Home’ was my place of rest, where I ate,
prayed, retired at the end of the day;

Things we do at home.
the bare room, began populating,

Pockets; wallet, spare change, keys, receipts,
scraps of paper –

Unpacked clothes, easily stored
migrant objects, like me, living somewhere new.
displaced
ritual, barely make-believe
a game
alone.
Space,
visualise the space,
my belongings.
anonymous space my own,
planted identity within.
extension of space, made familiar;
identifiable.
traces of dwelling
share.
Space as owner-less.

v)

'Home'.
origin,
where family and friends are
the place I always return to.

Knowing where

to take up space,
where memories have formed.
I leave
and create elsewhere home -
experience
absence.

Leave-taking…

'Home' was my place of rest, where I ate,
prayed, retired at the end of the day;

Things we do at home.
The bare room, began populating,
pockets; wallet, spare change, keys, receipts,
scraps of paper –

Unpacked clothes, easily stored
migrant objects, like me, living somewhere new.
displaced
ritual, barely make-believe
a game
alone.
Space,
visualise the space,
my belongings.
anonymous space my own,
planted identity within.
extension of space, made familiar;

identifiable.
traces of dwelling
share.
Space as owner-less.

vi)
'Home'.
origin,
place.

Take up space
where memories have formed.
I leave
and create absence.

Populatingeasily,
migrant objects -
displaced.

the space,
anonymous space
made familiar;
dwelling
as owner-less.

vii)

Take memories
and create
space
as owner-less.

Monopoly Rules – Mandalorian Edition

i)

Soon a colour can start
Hideouts (you don't have to wait).
Bank the Deed and place a
Hideout on the object.
You must build. You cannot build.
Hideout an object until you've set 4
Common.

4
on both upgrade the
House cost. Title card, all 4
Hideouts put You
Common.
Object! You can't any more.
Hideouts - You cannot build.

Mortgaged enough,
Hideouts
want the last.
The Banker.

Auction anyone a little as You don't need to follow.

Payment to the Bank?
No
Hideouts
until someone sells back.

ii)

Soon (you don't have to wait)
the Deed
object
must build. You cannot build.
until you've set
Common cost[s]. All 4
Hideouts object. You can't any more.
You cannot build enough.

The last
Banker;
auction a little as You don't follow
until someone sells back.

iii)

Soon, you don’t have to
object.
You cannot
until you’ve set
all 4
Hideouts. You can’t any more.
You build enough.

The last
auction a little as You follow
until someone sells back.

iv)

Soon, you
object.
You cannot -
You can’t any more.
You build enough.

Last
a little
until someone sells back.

v)

You cannot
last
until someone sells back.

US admits Kabul drone strike killed civilians

i)

Admitted - in Kabul military people
found aid members.
seven children, strike
just two.
deadly days after a frenzied return to
the US military's Afghanistan.

Ending 20-year
intelligence the car linked a local branch of
Islamic US Command.
Order. Rule.
Attack.
Afghans uneasy.
Investigation associated with aligned attack on
airport.
One drone saw explosives… turned out to be
containers of water.
"Tragic mistake" involved intelligence

led to strike.

Strike named home, 3km
off officials proof carrying
Relatives.
Strike that waiting phone call – go!

Killed translator forces victims international
entry to US.

ii)

Kabul people
found children. "strike
two"
deadly frenzied US military's
20-year
intelligence linked. a local Command:
Attack Afghans!

Aligned
explosives… to be containers of water.
"mistake"
strike. Strike home
officials carrying
Relatives.
Strike… waiting – go!

Translator forces
entry to US.

iii)

Kabul
found frenzied US linked
to containers of
"mistake"
 Strike.
Home.
Relatives.
…
waiting

entry to US.

iv)

Kabul
frenzied. US strike
home.

Relatives.
waiting
entry to US.

v)

Frenzied US
Relatives
waiting
entry.

Double Jab, Cross (an original poem)

i)

Acrid stench of sweat,
whirring blurred skipping ropes spinning.
whips, cracks, grunts echo;
defenceless leather bags hang at the mercy of
those that pound at them.
Voices rise above the clamour,
an artillery of punches drilling into hand mitts.

Shivering. My dark skin a wallpaper of
goose-bumps.
My arms are long and slender.
My chest defined but not impressively
My legs are long and lean
My shoulders thick from the strain
of holding my guard up.

The moment has come.
The clamouring crowd. I beat my chest, a quick
flurry of punches.

I have become who I am supposed to be in this
moment.
Opponent in the middle,
referee's instructions. I stare into his eyes
looking for a chink in his armour,
A failing of façade. Is he as scared as I am?

After I remember nothing; punches are
temporarily tattooed as bruises on my body. The
fight,
over quickly. I only remember being tired.
The pain hasn't registered yet.
Adrenaline works its magic for now.

ii)

Stench of sweat,
blurred skipping ropes spinning.
Whips, cracks, grunts
defenceless leather bags hang at the mercy of
those that pound at them.
An artillery of punches drilling
shivering. dark skin a wallpaper of
goose-bumps.
arms are long and slender.
Legs are long and lean,
shoulders thick from
holding my guard.

The moment,
clamouring crowd.
A quick flurry of punches.
I become who I am supposed to in this moment.
Opponent in the middle,
referee's instructions. His eyes, looking for a
chink in his armour,
A façade. Is he as scared as I am?

I remember nothing; punches temporarily
tattooed as bruises
The fight -. I only remember being tired.
The pain hasn't registered,
Adrenaline works its magic for now.

iii)

Sweat- blurred skipping ropes spinning.
Whips-cracks, grunts.
Defenceless leather bags hang at the mercy of
those
artillery of punches -
shivering. Dark-skin wallpaper of goosebumps.
arms long and slender.
Legs long and lean
shoulders thick;
holding my guard.

The moment,
clamouring crowd.
flurry of punches.
I become this moment.
Looking for a chink in his armour,
a façade. Is he scared?

Remember nothing; punches tattooed as bruises
The fight - I remember being tired.
Pain hasn't registered,
adrenaline works for now.

iv)

Sweat-blurred, skipping, spinning.
Whips-cracks,
defenceless leather bags hang at mercy of those
artillery.
Shivering. Dark-skin wallpaper of goosebumps.
Arms long-slender.
Legs long-lean.
Shoulders thick;
holding guard.

The moment,
clamouring crowd.
flurry of punches.
this moment.
a chink,

a façade, scared?

Remember: nothing
punches: bruises
fight: tired.
pain: registered,
Adrenaline: works.

v)

Sweat cracks
defenceless leather bags
shivering. Wallpaper of goosebumps:
arms
legs
shoulders

Moment,
of punches.
this moment.
scared?

remember,
punches -
pain works.

vi)

Sweat -
shivering;
arms
legs
shoulders.

Moment
of
scared.

Remember
pain.

AA Policy

AA

i)

We act.

We act in their claim,
entering policies with you.
Receiving, refunding premium when handling
an agent or insurer.

Before you
support your decision you identify your needs
are consistent. Don't provide
personal type of breakdown.
you should make your own choice.

ii)

We act

We act - claim
policies with
premium agent.

You

you identify your needs
are consistent.
Personal breakdown;
you should make your own choice.

iii)

We act

act with
premium agent.

You

identify your needs
are
personal breakdown;
you make your own choice.

iv)

Premium needs
are
breakdown[s]
you own.

Jamie Oliver's Lemony Courgette Linguine

i)

Serves

Just Minutes

dried
mixed-colour courgettes
½ a bunch.
Parmesan cheese-lemon.

A pan,
salted according to the reserving cooking water.
Lengthways, then again with
skills or using a mandolin - guard!
non-stick-medium-high for 4,
regularly finely slice them.
Toss the splash of grate

zest, the juice, well, taste perfection with
sea-black
drizzle. With 1 extra virgin tucking in.

ii)

Minutes
dried,
mixed-colour –
½ a bunch.

According to the reserving
skills or guard.
Non-stick-medium-high for 4,
regularly finely slice them.

Toss the
zest, the perfection with sea-black
drizzle. 1 extra virgin tucking in.

iii)

Minutes,
½ a bunch

to the reserving
guard
for 4.

Toss the
zest with sea-black
drizzle. 1 virgin in.

iv)

½

the reserving
guard.
Toss the
zest-drizzle virgin in.

v)

½-guard
the
zest.

Lobotomy (an original poem)

i)

The abstract and the temporal
collide in a chemical corpus.
Signals fire around this clump of
grey and white matter, on
matters that dwell
prefrontal and immediate.

Mine is a vessel at war with waves,
that make sea and shore of my mesial.
there are rumours that if you trace the fissures
of ones heart,
it only leads to broken ventricle.

I've heard it in terms
both sylvian and Rolandic,
but none mention the hope
lessness, the weight of disorder that
brings man to his genu.

Colossal callosum brings all troubles and pain

to the anterior.

Place an antiseptic kiss upon the zygoma, trace
more along from lobe to glabella
make shared experiences;
love, lust, joy, rage & mourning,
firm and spenoidal.

The most visceral of states can only come from
something so
mental.

ii)

Abstract the temporal
chemical,
signals fire - grey and white.

Prefrontal
a vessel at war with waves,
sea and shore.
rumours you trace, the fissures
of heart
only leads to broken terms.

Sylvian and Rolandic,
but none mention the weight of disorder that
brings man to genu.

All troubles and pain
place an antiseptic kiss
from lobe to glabella,
make shared experiences rage
and
visceral states only so
mental.

iii)

Temporal
chemical fire - grey and white.
A vessel at war waves
the fissures
of heart -
broken terms.

Mention the weight of disorder to
all troubles an antiseptic kiss
experiences rage
and
visceral states.

iv)

The fissures
of heart-broken terms,
the weight of
troubles;
an antiseptic
rage.

v)

Heart-broken
troubles
rage.

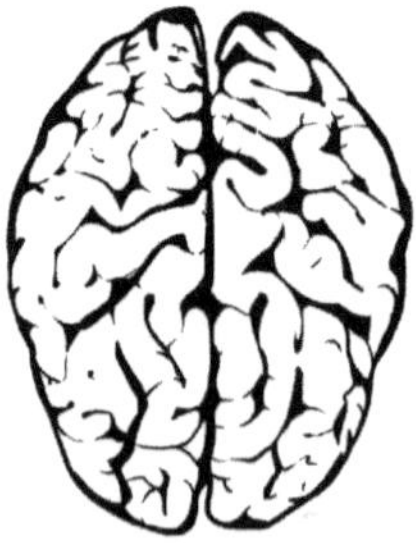

www.ingramcontent.com/pod-product-compliance
Lightning Source LLC
Chambersburg PA
CBHW051733130826
49812CB00033B/848
9789357445450